for dreamers...

ISBN: 978-0-9800123-2-3

Printed in the United States by Morris Publishing®
3212 East Highway 30
Kearney, NE 68847
1-800-650-7888

7 steps to dream followin'

Hey! Dreams Come True

Dreams come differently,
in all sorts of sorts.
Some come tall and lofty,
while others come up short.

Dreams can come from inside,
in all kinds of kinds.
Some come in your heart,

others come in your mind.

Dreams can come from outside,
in all ways of ways.
Some carried in bags by birds,

others pulled by sleighs.

Dreams can come while you sleep,
in all types of types.
Some come with polka dots,

others come with stripes.

Dreams can come if you love,
in all forms of forms.
Some come completely alone,

others come in swarms.

Dreams can come drifting by,
in all styles of styles.
Some up the Mississippi,

others down the Nile.

Dreams can come differently,
to me and to you.
but as long as we believe...

Hey! Scratch that itch

I went to the doctor right after soccer.
And said to him, What's up doc?

I have this itch that's been making me twitch?
And it's been itching me 'round the clock.

Bugs in your bed? A hat on your head?
Chickenpox under your chin?

A snake down your shirt? Grass in your skirt?
Or poison ivy all over your skin?

Those make me itch, but not like this.
This itch hasn't turned red.

It's more of an itch that turns on the switch,
to the light upstairs in my head.

Cake on your plate? Staying up late?
Stuffed animals bigger than you?

Video games? Books with weird names?
Or things that can turn your tongue blue?

Closer I think, to finding the thing,
the thing that burns in my heart.

It makes me feel like my ideas are ideal.
It makes me feel like I'm smart.

Hmmm, said the doc, it's not as I thought.
It's bigger than that it seems.

This itch that you've got, we don't see a lot.
You've got a case of The Dreams!

Oh no, The Dreams? What does that mean?
Am I a goner for sure?

What do I do? I haven't a clue.
Doc, is there even a cure?

Think of this thing that's making you dream,
the same thing that's making you twitch.

Then do that thing, dream that dream,
and be sure to scratch that itch.

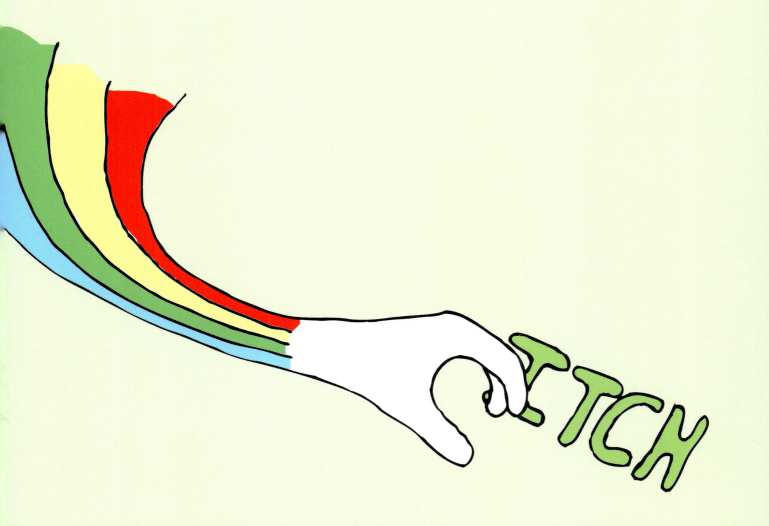

Hey! Get Off The Couch

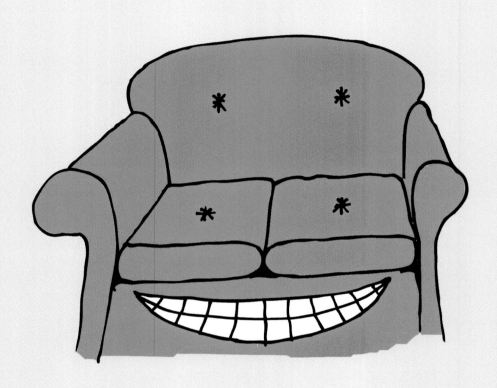

I sat on the couch and just as I slouched, something bit my bum.

Could it be? Oh yes indeed!
The couch had teeth and gums.

Mr. couch, I don't mean to grouch,
but did you just chew my cheek?

Indeed I did Mr. kid.
You and I need to speak.

What the what, that's nuts!
Do I believe my ears?

Since when do couches talk?
And since when do they bite rears?

I'm not a normal couch, he said.
I'm a couch coach, you see.

I coach kids to get off the couch,
instead of sitting on me.

I tickle, I tweak, I squeeze and I squash.
I punch, I pinch and I pull.

I make people get off the couch,
and fill their dream cups full.

Sorry silly sofa, I said,
but I really need to rest.

Besides, I need to sleep to dream.
That's how I dream best.

I'm afraid that's out of order.
I simply can't let you sleep.

I'm your guide to get outside,
not lay here and count the sheep.

Fine! I said, I'll sleep on the floor, nothing you can do about that.

So I sat on the ground and laid my head down, until I was completely flat.

You look like lumber trying to slumber.
You'll never reach dreams at this pace.

All of your dreams wont happen it seems.
You'll just stare off into space.

The couch was right, my mind took flight,
and seemed to wishfully wander.

I could not sleep. Not even a wink.
So I stared into space to ponder.

How big is space? Is it a place?
Or does it go on forever?

I've always wanted to go into space, ya know?
I should go on a space adventure!

That's when I knew, my dream could come true,
if I chased it all the way.

Guess what Mr. Couch that made me say ouch?
I will go to space one day!

Jolly good, as you should, said the couch,
as I ran out to chase my new dream.

So did I make it to space? Well let's just say,
the view from the moon is supreme.

Hey! Don't Act Your Age

You could wear big, circus shoes,
and juggle like a clown.

Or you could wear disco ball shoes,
and dance all around town.

You could choose gator boots,
and cruise through puddles and ponds.

Or you could choose magic shoes,
fly on a broom and little broom wands.

You might fancy mountain spikes,
to climb the Tallest Peak.

Or you might fancy no shoes at all,
to surf any wave you seek.

How about cop shoes-with-shoes-with-shoes,
to chase down a fleeing crook?

Or how about socks as shoes,
to snuggle up with a book?

Why not try hover shoes,
and spend your days out travelin'?

Or why not try new-sport shoes,
and invent the Rainbow Javelin?

You could choose a million shoes,
and do a million things.

You could go a million places,
and meet a million kings.

But wherever you decide to go,
and whatever you decide to do,

don't act your age, my friend.
Act the size of your shoe.

Hey! Have The Day You're Gonna Have

Today is a day,
that much we know.
But what kind of day,
only time will show.

Things are going to happen,
things good and things bad.
Things are going to happen
on this day you have not yet had.

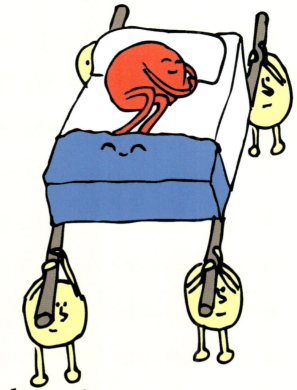

Mom might let you sleep in,
and go late to school.

Or she might wake you early,
and have you clean the pool.

Breakfast could be delicious,
Pancakes, waffles and more.

Or it could be an awful protein shake,
that shakes your very core.

Perhaps Dad will drive you to school
in his awesome, brand-new car.

Or perhaps you'll miss the bus,
and have to walk so very far.

Possibly you'll find a dollar,
or maybe you'll find ten.

Or possibly you'll lose some money,
but never remember when.

Maybe your teacher will hang your picture
high up on the wall.

Or maybe you'll trip on the easel,
spill the paint and fall.

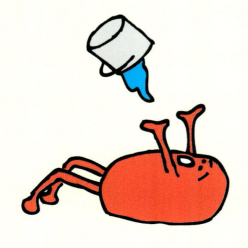

Lunch could be as yummy,
as a fancy restaurant feast.

Or it could be a nightmare,
featuring the Tuna Beast.

During afternoon recess,
you may score the winning goal.

Or recess may be rained out,
and the afternoon may be dull.

**Maybe school will end early,
giving you hours of time to play.**

**Or maybe school will be longer,
and you'll have to do homework all day.**

You might race friends and win,
on your bike ride home.

Or you might have two flat tires
and have to walk home all alone.

A lot of things could happen today,
on this day of days unknown.

But one thing you should know for sure,
is that a smile can always be shown.

So have the day you're going to have,
and let come what may.

Because it's up to you to say,
today is going to be a...

good day

Hey! Smile More

People are smiling
all over the earth.
Each smile is unique.
And each has great worth.

But the world can be scary
and full of nasty things.
Sometimes people get lonely
and forget to say cheese.

Some places have less sunshine
shining on down.
So people do the worst kind of thing.
People frown.

But never you fear, my friends.
And never you worry.
There's a trick up your sleeve
to save the world in a hurry.

It's a superpower you have
and your friends can have it too.
Just tell them to follow after you
and do as you do.

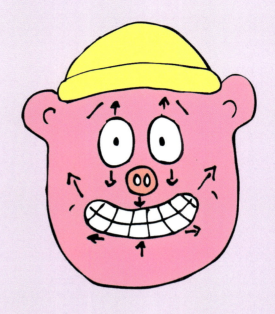

Make your eyes big, teeth clenched
and lips really wide.
Lift the corners of your mouth
to your ears on either side.

Your superpower is called

smiling

So smile as much as you can.
Your superpower is working.
It's shining from here to Japan.

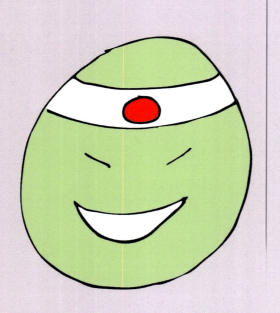

It's shining to the moon and back,
it's shining to the stars.
It's also shining on your friends,
those near and those far.

It's shining on the dark places
where the sun can't always be.
It's shining on the monsters,
turning them into funky trees.

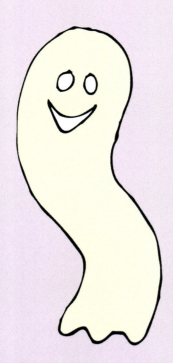

It's shining on the ghosts and goblins,
shining away all the creepy.
It's shining on the feisty creatures
and making them all sleepy.

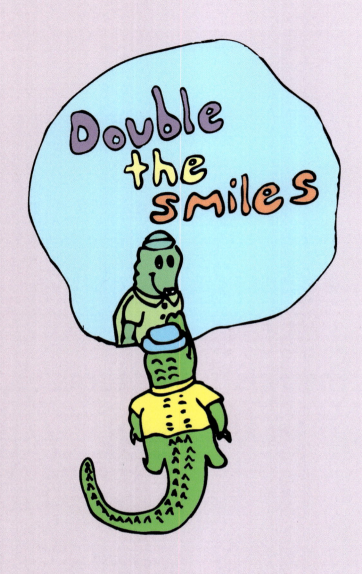

Your smile glows in the dark.
And it shines on crocodiles.
It shines on your own reflection
and creates double the smiles.

It shines on your family,
whoever they may be.
It makes them happier
and turns you and I into we.

Your smile can make grown-ups laugh
or make you warm when it's chilly.
Or it can help out the angry
who are mad about something silly.

So if you see some people
who don't want to play.
Shine your smile in their direction
and brighten up their day.

Smile big and smile wide.
Smile high and smile low.
Smiling is a superpower
so be sure to

Hey! Follow Your Dreams

Here comes the Dream Bus,
cruising up the street.

Better wave it down,
jump in and take a seat.

Put on your dreamin' shoes
and pack a bag full of laughter.

Prepare for the unknown
and get ready for ever after.

dreamin' shoes

You're going to need a seatbelt
cause it will be a wild ride.
The Dream Bus will take you out there,
to places far and places wide.

You will hit bumps and make turns,
you will speed up and slow down.

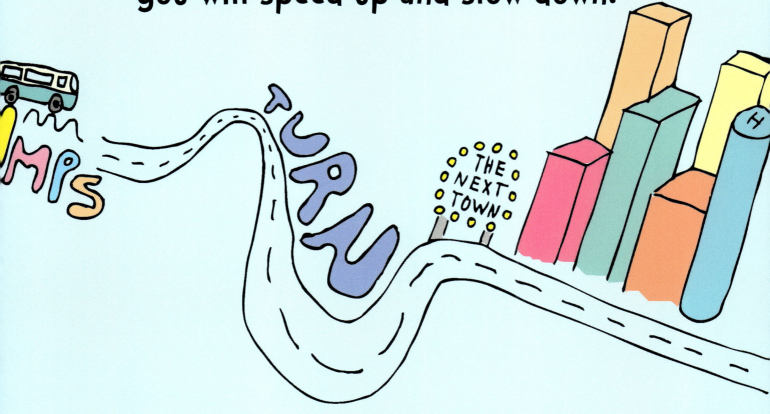

You will remember the road behind,
but look forward to the next town.

Don't be scared of the cliffs
and don't look over the ledge.

The Dream Bus might seem out of control,
but it's just driving on the edge.

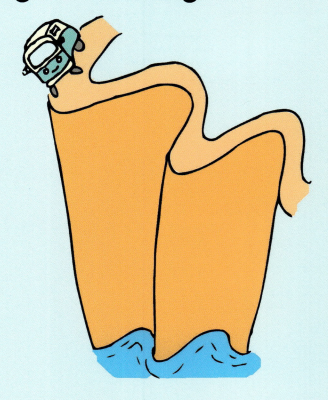

You're on your way to do it,
whatever it is you love most.
You're not doing it for the money,
and you're not doing it to boast.

You are doing it cause you love it.
So even if it gets rough,
remember you are on The Dream Bus
and dreaming can be tough.